FRIEND OF THE POOR
MARY AIKENHEAD

Rosaleen Crossan

FRIEND OF THE POOR
MARY AIKENHEAD

Woman of Vision, Commitment and Inspiration

the columba press

First published in 2016 by
the columba press
a division of Grace Communications Ltd,
23 Merrion Square, Dublin 2

Cover design by Helene Pertl | The Columba Press
Cover image of Mary Aikenhead © Religious Sisters of Charity
Origination by The Columba Press
Printed by ScandBook AB, Sweden

Scripture References from the Jerusalem Bible, Popular Edition

ISBN 978 1 78218 280 1

Contents

✳✳✳✳✳✳✳✳✳✳✳✳✳✳✳✳✳✳✳✳

A Mustard Seed

Neither the planter nor the waterer matters:
only God who makes things grow.

1 Co 3:7

And certainly, the small seed that Mary Aikenhead planted back in 1815 as foundress of the Religious Sisters of Charity has flourished, blossomed and expanded beyond her wildest dreams, simply because of her total dedication and absolute trust in God's Providence at work in the congregation.

Most great ventures begin with the vision of an individual, and Mary Aikenhead's ambition to give 'to the poor what the rich can buy for money' became a reality because she trusted the dream of God in her heart. The story of this young girl, whose brave spirit dared to break a new furrow in poverty-stricken Ireland in the nineteenth century, proves the power of one when impelled by the spirit of God and an indomitable will.

Mary Aikenhead followed her dream, in spite of many challenges, planting her seed of compassion for the poor and destitute by founding the Religious Sisters of Charity in 1815. Happily, she lived to see the congregation expand and gain momentum through her selfless commitment and love for the poor, aided by like-minded young women of her day.

On her deathbed Mary exclaimed: 'After I am gone, the congregation will flourish.'

These prophetic words took root and the result is visible today in the many areas at home and abroad where the Religious Sisters of Charity minister to people in every kind of need.

The mustard seed which Mary planted has indeed become a large and expansive tree, with countless branches reaching out to those who are in need of compassion and care in our modern, sophisticated, yet in many ways deprived and lonely world.

PART I

****

The Story of a Life

Every person's story is as unique as his/her fingerprints. Some lives may be ordinary and uneventful, reminiscent of a calm, serene lake; others may be exciting and awe-inspiring like the powerful energy of a waterfall. St Paul states: 'The life and death of each of us has its influence on others' (Rm 14:7), so inevitably, every life leaves an imprint on humanity whether it be small or great. Mary Aikenhead's story reveals the extent of her influence on the society of her time, an influence which continues to have an extensive ripple effect on a global scale today.

Beginnings

Mary Aikenhead was born on 19 January 1787 in the city of Cork in an era when the majority of Catholics were struggling to survive following the harsh and restrictive penal laws which had crippled them for so long. Mary's father was Dr David Aikenhead, a Protestant and a medical practitioner who ran a chemist shop under the trade name of Aikenhead and Dupont. Her mother, Mary Stackpole, the daughter of a Catholic merchant in the city, was a Catholic. Although Mary's mother was free to practise her religion, she was not allowed under the Protestant Church laws to rear her family as Catholics. This explains why Mary was brought to the Protestant Church for baptism. Following the ceremony, Mary, who was sickly at birth, was fostered out to a devout Catholic couple, John and Mary Rorke, who lived in a cottage on Eason's Hill, a semi-rural site overlooking the city. Here,

Mary would get an abundance of the fresh air she so badly needed.

It is widely known that the first six years of a child's life are crucial in determining the future strengths and weaknesses of that child. In Mary's case, her personality can be traced back to two strands in her experience of early nurturance. Firstly, Mary and John Rorke, or Mammy and Daddy Rorke as Mary called them, were blessed with a deep faith and trust in God and they involved Mary in all their religious observances. Mary prayed the rosary every night on Mammy Rorke's knees and she accompanied her foster parents to Mass in the North Chapel every Sunday morning. The little girl was fascinated by all the statues and stained-glass windows and the fragrant smell of incense inside the North Chapel.

Secondly, the families among whom Mary lived and played on Eason's Hill were poor and they struggled to feed and clothe their children. We must remember that Mary came from a privileged background where want was never experienced. How often the little girl must have wondered, as she played with her young friends on cold winter days, why she had nice warm boots and a cosy woollen coat while many of her little playmates wore ragged jumpers, cotton dresses and very shabby footwear. However, it is well documented that Dr Aikenhead was liberally generous to the poor, never charging them for sick calls or medicine, and no doubt the families on Eason's Hill would have benefited from his generosity.

Looking at those two strands in Mary's early days – a devout Catholic experience and a first-hand knowledge of how the poor lived – we see seeds planted within her which would bear fruit in the future foundress of the Sisters of Charity.

Mary's parents brought her back to the family home when she was six years of age. She now had two younger sisters and a brother soon to be born. Fortunately for Mary, she did not have to experience a heart-wrenching separation from her Mammy and Daddy Rorke, since David Aikenhead employed Mary Rorke as nurse to the children and John became the doctor's coach driver.

✳✳✳✳✳✳✳✳✳✳✳✳✳✳✳✳✳✳✳✳✳✳✳✳✳✳✳✳✳✳

Mary was now living in what could be considered a luxurious home in Daunt's Square, where fires blazed in every room and two nursery maids looked after the children. We may be sure that little Mary's heart often bled as she snuggled into a warm, cosy bed every night and thought about her little friends on the hill whose lives were so different from her own.

Early Years

Dr Aikenhead organised that Mary begin her education with the children of Protestant gentlemen where all were educated in the rubrics of the gentry. On Sundays Mary attended the Protestant services with her father and she must have wondered why there were no bells, and no red light in the sanctuary as in the North Chapel. She deeply missed attending Mass on Sunday with Mammy and Daddy Rorke, but her sensitive heart wished not to upset her beloved father.

When Mary was twelve, Dr Aikenhead put his business up for sale and moved his family to Rutland Street on the south side of the city. It was here that, providentially, Mary's aunt Mrs Rebecca Gorman, her mother's widowed sister, came from France to live with her relatives in the city. Mrs Gorman, a deeply religious lady, was to have a huge influence on Mary's life.

✳✳✳✳✳✳✳✳✳✳✳✳✳✳✳✳✳✳✳✳✳✳✳✳✳✳✳✳✳✳✳

One day Mary accompanied her aunt to Mass and, as it happened, that day Benediction of the Blessed Sacrament followed the Mass. This experience moved Mary deeply, and on hearing an explanation of the rite from her aunt, Mary's thirst for more knowledge of the Catholic faith was deepened. From this time onwards Mary began to slip out of home to attend morning Mass and devotions.

Sadness hit the Aikenhead household when David Aikenhead took seriously ill over Christmas in 1801. There being no hope for his recovery, he asked for a priest, who received him into the Catholic Church. He died peacefully on 28 December with his loving family and friends around his bed.

Not long after her father's death, Mary, attending Mass in the South Chapel, heard Dr Florence McCarthy, the coadjutor bishop of Cork, preach on the parable of the rich man and Lazarus (Lk 16:19–31). Mary was very struck by the story of the rich man who wallowed in his luxuries and totally ignored the poor man at his gate, never sharing with him even a crumb from his table. The poor man goes to heaven; the rich man does not. We can well imagine that Mary, living as she was in relative luxury, and at the same time witnessing many starving poor on the streets around her in the city, took deeply to heart the message from Jesus that the poor are God's favoured children and the rich have an obligation to share their blessings with them. Small wonder that Mary's *raison d'être* for the congregation of the Sisters of Charity would later be: 'To give to the poor what the rich can buy for money.'

This parable of the rich man and Lazarus was to define the rest of Mary's life. Her experience of attending Mass and Catholic devotions with her aunt also touched her soul and reignited within her the childhood feelings for and attraction to the Catholic religion. On one occasion she announced to her aunt: 'I shall never be happy until I am a Catholic.' Her aunt immediately seized the opportunity and set about organising a course of instruction in the Catholic faith for Mary, who afterwards was received into the Catholic Church on 6 June 1802 at the age of fifteen. Shortly after this her two sisters, Anne and Margaret, and her little brother, St John, also became Catholics.

A New Dawn

After her father's death, Mary stepped in to help her mother with the financial running of the house as well as keeping a good eye on her three younger siblings. Again, Providence was at work as this experience of managing finance enabled Mary to become an astute businesswoman, a quality necessary in her future role as mother general.

As a teenager, Mary had many trips to make throughout the city to secure business deals. Passing the poor begging on the streets day after day must have haunted her heart and reminded her of the parable which had engraved itself in her mind. Mary decided to do something about the situation, so, enlisting the help of her good friend Cecelia Lynch, she collected food and clothes from their rich, young friends; then both young women climbed rickety stairs and visited the hovels in the back lanes to distribute to poor families whatever they could give them.

✳✳✳✳✳✳✳✳✳✳✳✳✳✳✳✳✳✳✳✳✳✳✳✳✳✳✳✳✳✳

Like all teenagers, Mary was interested in the social life of her times. She frequently attended balls, concerts and other social events with her young friends. However, since becoming a Catholic, Mary seldom missed daily Mass and it was said by an early biographer that 'she burned down a whole mould candle while saying her prayers'.

No great work was ever done for God except by persons of prayer.

About this time, Mary was also toying with the idea of becoming a nun. She had a deep conviction that she was called to give her life to God in a religious order, but she also felt equally convinced of the call to help alleviate the plight of the suffering poor. The only religious Mary knew in Cork were the Ursuline and the Presentation orders and both were bound by the rule of enclosure. Mary was in a dilemma!

✳✳✳✳✳✳✳✳✳✳✳✳✳✳✳✳✳✳✳✳✳✳✳✳✳✳✳✳✳✳

Providence, however, was to intervene once again through a chance meeting with Mrs Anna Maria O'Brien in the Ursuline convent in Cork. Both young women soon discovered that concern for the poor was a bond uniting them and, since Mary had recently received an invitation from her friend Cecelia Lynch to her profession in the Poor Clare convent in Harold's Cross, Dublin, Anna Maria invited her to stay at her home while in Dublin. Cecelia Lynch had pleaded with Mary not to make up her mind about her future as a religious until she should experience the profession ceremony in the Poor Clares. Cecelia may have hoped that Mary would join her there as a Poor Clare sister. Providence, however, ordained otherwise through this meeting with Anna Maria.

Consequently, Anna Maria O'Brien was to have a huge influence on the turn of events in Mary's life. Anna Maria, like Mary, had organised other young women to visit the sick and the poor in their homes in Dublin and Fr Daniel Murray, coadjutor bishop of Dublin, later to become archbishop, was assisting Anna Maria in this ministry as well as being her spiritual guide. Daniel Murray was a man of deep compassion and his concern for the poor in Dublin was such that he hoped to found a religious order that would specifically look after them. Anna Maria planned that this great friend of hers would be present at her home when Mary visited. We can imagine Mary's great delight on hearing the plans of Dr Murray. It was her own dream that an order of nuns be found who would not be bound by enclosure and so be enabled to look after the poor in their homes. Mary was so enthused that she told him she would join such an order should he find an efficient leader.

On a subsequent visit to Dublin, much to Mary's joy, Daniel Murray proclaimed he had found a worthy leader. Her joy was dashed, however, when she learned that she herself was the person he had chosen having observed her deep-seated love for the poor during their last encounter. Mary was dumbfounded, saying she would never be able to carry such a responsibility. Only when Dr Murray told her he was sure that this was God's will for her did Mary accept the offer to become the leader, provided she be given adequate training. Plans were soon put in place to have Mary and a companion, Alicia Walsh, undertake a three-year period of training in the manner of religious life in the noviciate of the Institute of the Blessed Virgin Mary in the Bar convent, York, England.

It was in the Bar convent that Mary was introduced to the spirituality of St Ignatius, founder of the Jesuit Order, as the sisters in York lived according to his rule, adapted for religious women. Later, when Mary was seeking to establish constitutions for the Sisters of Charity, she chose the York rule from among others she had studied as the most favourable for the new congregation.

We should indeed try to be children of prayer and living emblems of perfect Conformity to the Most Holy and Divine Will.

The Fledgling Congregation

On 22 August 1815, Mary, now known as Mother Mary Augustine Aikenhead, and her companion, now Mother Mary Catherine Walsh, accompanied by their saintly guide Dr Daniel Murray, arrived in North William Street, Dublin to begin their ministry as Sisters of Charity in the orphanage where fourteen young children eagerly awaited them.

On 1 September 1815, both young women took their vows of poverty, chastity and obedience for one year; added to these was the fourth vow of service of the poor. Dr Murray believed they needed the year to organise a rule for their way of life. Mary later confided to a friend that the vows she had taken that day were, in her mind, her final vows. The vow to serve the poor is a distinguishing characteristic of the Sisters of Charity and it links back to the fifteen-year-old Mary in the South Chapel,

Cork, when she responded to the call of God to serve the poor as she listened to the story of Dives and Lazarus.

Having taken their vows, Dr Murray placed the sisters under the spiritual care of Fr Peter Kenney SJ, whose invaluable wisdom and guidance to Mary and the sisters was to continue for many years to come. In 1817, preaching the sermon at a Mass when two candidates were receiving the habit, Fr Kenney took as his theme *Caritas Christi Urget Nos* – the charity of Christ urges us on (2 Co 5:14). Such was the impact of these words and their relevance to the mission of the infant congregation, from that day onwards it became the motto for the new congregation.

> *Sisters of Charity are not to gain Heaven*
> *without suffering with as well as for the poor.*

✳✳✳✳✳✳✳✳✳✳✳✳✳✳✳✳✳✳✳✳✳✳✳✳✳✳✳✳✳✳✳

The people of North William Street were so happy to see Mary and Catherine walking the streets and visiting the poor in their homes that they called them 'the Walking Nuns'. The attraction of Mary and Catherine's dedication to the poor soon brought many a knock on the convent door as aspiring young women enthusiastically offered themselves to become part of the great enterprise which was the Sisters of Charity. Many of these young women gave up very comfortable situations at home in order to serve the poor. We can imagine the sacrifice involved in adapting to a very different, frugal way of life, as in those early days there were occasions when a bowl of oatmeal porridge was the main meal two days a week.

Looking after the orphans, teaching in a nearby school, and visiting the sick and destitute in their homes were some of the tasks undertaken by the sisters.

As the number of sisters began to swell, Mary needed to look for extra accommodation. Eventually she and another professed sister, along with seven novices and postulants, moved to Stanhope Street, where they continued their ministry in the nearby school and hospital. Mary undertook the training of the novices herself and she also accompanied the young sisters on their visits to the sick poor, where they learned from her the respect and compassion necessary in the heart of a Sister of Charity. Mary was often heard to say that there was no charity where there was no respect for the poor.

Mary Aikenhead's absolute trust in God is evident in the many challenges she faced while ministering to the poor. During the outbreak of the Asiatic cholera which visited Dublin in 1832, Mary, trusting in God's protection, did not hesitate to send her young sisters, some of them yet novices, to the temporary hospital in Grangegorman Lane, where as many as eight patients per bed would die over the course of a single day. Every morning a new list of the names of the dead would be posted on the hospital gate, usually numbering between fifty and eighty. Mary's trust in Divine Providence was rewarded, and only one sister contracted the illness, but afterwards

✳✳✳✳✳✳✳✳✳✳✳✳✳✳✳✳✳✳✳✳✳✳✳✳✳✳✳✳✳✳

recovered. In these early days, however, much to Mary's sorrow, she lost some of the young members of the Order to tuberculosis, then known as consumption.

> *We should be wanting in gratitude to our good*
> *and merciful Lord if we did not entrust*
> *all our concerns with unlimited confidence.*

.

Expansion

As the number of sisters increased so did the number of requests for new foundations of Sisters of Charity. In 1826 Mary travelled to Cork to oversee arrangements for a new community in her native city. It was now fourteen years since Mary had left her home and her joy was immense when the first person to greet her as she alighted from the carriage was Daddy John. Mary's dream of having a foundation in Cork was soon to be realised.

The new convent proposed by the bishop was quite dilapidated and the sisters good-humouredly named their new home 'Cork Castle'. Four sisters, including Mary's sister Anne, who had joined the congregation in 1822, began their work of visiting the poor in the North Parish. Conditions were horrendous at this time in the city as typhus fever raged and infection was rampant. The sisters worked tirelessly for the relief of the poor, but paid a

✳✳✳✳✳✳✳✳✳✳✳✳✳✳✳✳✳✳✳✳✳✳✳✳✳✳✳✳✳✳✳✳✳

heavy price, as Anne Aikenhead caught typhus, which later developed into consumption. Mary brought her sister back to Stanhope Street convent where she could help care for her, but sadly Anne died on 8 August 1828. We can only imagine the sorrow and sense of loss that Mary suffered.

To this day the sisters remain in Cork, where they are involved in education, parish ministry and social care of women who are mentally challenged.

A few years after the Cork foundation, Archbishop Murray requested a school to be managed by the Sisters of Charity in Gardiner Street. The Archbishop, having received a bequest, set about the building of a new convent and an adjoining school, both of which were opened in 1830. Mary Aikenhead always held that there should be a school for poor children wherever there was a convent and the school at Gardiner Street was to be the first school in Dublin run by the Sisters of Charity.

※※※※※※※※※※※※※※※※※※※※※※※※※※※※※※

It is obvious that we shall have a greater
number of schools than of any other
institutions for the poor.

Mary's cousin, Sr Mary Xavier Hennessy, took over
the running of the school. Gifted as she was in school
management, Sr Xavier found the hundreds of eager
young girls, who may have had more interest in the free
breakfast than in the free education, too big a handful to
manage. Mary suggested she enlist the help of a Christian
Brother, and Edmund Rice willingly lent her Br Duggan,
a gifted teacher who was to prove priceless in sharing his
method of organising classes and controlling pupils. With
his assistance, Gardiner Street school went from strength
to strength and today continues to offer the very best in
education to the young boys and girls in that part of the
city.

One year later, another foundation was made at
Sandymount at the request of a charitable lady, Barbara

Verschoyle, who was building a convent and a school for the poor. Apart from teaching in the school, the sisters were also involved in visiting the poor and the sick in the surrounding villages. Poverty was rampant in Sandymount at this time. Small wonder that in 1832 the Asiatic cholera broke out, causing untold hardship among the poor. Mary used an old store as a temporary hospital, where the sisters tirelessly attended the sick.

Other foundations followed, notably Donnybrook Castle in 1837. The castle was purchased to provide a home for the women from the penitent asylum in Townsend Street. The sisters had taken over from Mrs Ryan, a niece of Archbishop Troy, who was no longer able to care for them.

Probably one of the most trusting and generous actions of Mary Aikenhead was her acceptance of a request from Bishop Polding OSB in Australia to send Sisters of Charity to Parramatta, Sydney, to help the women convicts in the prison. This was at a time when Mary could ill afford to sacrifice sisters for a foreign mission due to the demands at home. However, the plight of the women convicts touched Mary's heart, so without hesitation and trusting in Divine Providence she asked for volunteers for this challenging mission. Five sisters generously offered themselves and, despite her poor health, Mary accompanied the sisters to Dún Laoghaire on 12 August 1838 and sadly waved them goodbye. The arrival in Australia of these five brave, pioneering women would go down in history, as these were the first religious sisters to set foot on Australian soil.

The sisters were invited to work with the eight hundred women and three hundred children confined in the prison. The women were involved in the outdoor manual labour of breaking stones and sawing wood. We can well imagine the effect of this work on the behaviour of the prisoners, who jostled each other and used foul language. The sisters strongly believed that the women's lives would change for the better if they were given more refined work. Advocating on their behalf, they succeeded in getting the authorities to allow the women to do needlework and laundry. Such was the change that eventually the women were receiving wages for their indoor work. The ministry of the sisters was not confined to the prison, as they also instructed children in the local schools, visited the men in prison awaiting execution and visited the sick in hospital.

Unfortunately, distance from Ireland meant that these Sisters of Charity would become a separate congregation. Before long, however, the congregation began to flourish as new members were attracted. Today the sisters in Australia continue to live out the charism of Mary Aikenhead in hospitals, schools and other diverse ministries; and thanks to advances in technology and travel, the two congregations maintain a close relationship, sharing in each other's gatherings and missions.

We each and all must try our best to stand steady under the heat and burden of the day, and with perseverance, labour in our special engagements in service of the poor.

In Mary's lifetime other foundations were made, including St Vincent's Hospital in St Stephen's Green, Waterford City, Clarinbridge, Co. Galway, where soup kitchens were set up during the Great Famine, Clonmel, Co. Tipperary, Preston in England and Harold's Cross, where Mary spent the final days of her life.

Some of these foundations still exist today and the sisters, their colleagues and volunteers continue in the footsteps of Mary Aikenhead to serve the vulnerable and needy, who, in spite of the varied government services, experience the need of a fellow human to ease the pain of challenges thrown up by modern-day living. How truly Jesus said, 'you have the poor with you always' (Jn 12:8).

> *We must prepare and be willing to labour*
> *for the poor in our vocation.*

A Dream Within a Dream

Once Mary's vision of a congregation to serve the poor was achieved, another dream close to her heart came to the fore. Mary had, from the very beginning, nurtured a desire to set up a hospital for the sole purpose of providing the best medical care to the poor, who could never afford to access such services.

Any great venture carries a price tag and certainly Mary had to pay dearly to see her dream come true. Almost all of her friends considered her totally misguided, saying she had neither money nor personnel to run a hospital. Writing to her great friend, Mother Mary de Chantal, in the Cork convent, Mary laments: 'We have not, or seem not to have, anyone but the Almighty Himself to aid us in this great undertaking ... All this want of support, this falling away of everyone is a trial to me ... [b]ut *all, all* is far from proving that the good work is not His.'

Mary persevered in her conviction that it was God's work and her confidence was rewarded when the money required to buy what was once the Earl of Meath's mansion in St Stephen's Green was kindly given by a new member to the congregation. Where personnel was concerned, Providence stepped in when Dr O'Ferrall, a very able physician with a great heart for the poor, promised to assist Mary in every way possible with the running of the hospital.

Mary wanted the very best and up-to-date medical care for the poor so, daringly, pushing out further boundaries, she sent three Sisters of Charity to Paris to study the manner of managing hospitals under the system of the Hospitalières of St Thomas of Villanova. This was the first time in Ireland that a hospital would be run by Catholic women. A saying attributed to Mary Aikenhead reveals her ability to think outside the box.

> *Just because it was never done before,*
> *doesn't mean it cannot be done now.*

****

Eyebrows were raised and much gossip abounded when it was learned that the new hospital was to be located in St Stephen's Green, the favourite residence of the elite. Mary persisted in her aim, saying nothing was too good for God's elite – the suffering poor. For the poor, Mary laboured unstintingly and she herself cut up the linen for all the sheets and pillowcases. Being confined to bed with acute pain at this time did not deter her from sewing with her own hands the bolster and pillow slips for the future hospital.

It is interesting that the second physician appointed by Mary was Dr Bellingham, a Protestant from a decidedly anti-Catholic family.

Against all the obstacles, then, Mary's dream was fulfilled and St Vincent's Hospital in St Stephen's Green opened its doors on 23 January 1834 to the poor of Dublin regardless of sect or creed. In later years Mary often wrote in her letters that because of her many benefactors 'St Vincent's was a continuous miracle of Divine Providence'. Mary herself was in no small way responsible for the 'continuous miracle' through her many long hours of writing begging notes – 3,500 in all – which she sent out before Christmas in 1836. We can only guess the hardship this involved for Mary, who at this time was bedridden with painful arthritis, yet she worked till 3 a.m. getting letters ready for delivery the next day.

Mary's interest in St Vincent's Hospital and her dedication to its well-being continued until the end of her life. It is without dispute that St Vincent's Hospital would never have come into being without the determination, the absolute selflessness and the sheer conviction of Mary that the poor deserved the very best in healthcare. Blessed Edmund Rice, founder of the Christian Brothers, said of Mary:

She is such a woman as God raises up once in a hundred years, when there is a great work to be done.

It is Accomplished

Mary Aikenhead was only forty-four years old when her life became dogged by ill-health. Yet she persevered in her role as leader of the congregation, and even when confined to her bedroom received many dignitaries and other important contacts who helped support the work on behalf of the poor.

The cause of Mary's ill health was acute arthritis, which often so disabled her that she was unable to leave her bed. Constant headaches also added to her discomfort. Undaunted, as ever, Mary continued to plan and organise the leaders of the new foundations who required her advice and sound judgement.

Eventually, Mary's health became a cause for alarm, as cold winter months brought on frequent bouts of bronchitis, which left her in a very weakened state. Living in St Vincent's Hospital necessitated climbing long stretches of stairs which Mary was no longer able to manage.

In Harold's Cross, a spacious house, which had a large garden with surrounding fields, came on the market. This house was purchased as it would make a suitable noviciate and Mary would benefit from the fresh air that such a change would bring. Consequently, on 11 September 1845, Mary moved to Harold's Cross where she was now able to avail of the sunshine and fresh air out of doors. Having the novices around her was a joy to Mary and they in turn benefited from her many conversations and spiritual wisdom. We can imagine the light-heartedness the novices brought as they laughed and joked and lifted Mary's heart while wheeling her around the grounds in her bath chair. It is reported that on one occasion a novice jostled the bath chair and tipped Mary onto the ground. With immense difficulty the novices managed to get Mary back into the chair, no doubt causing her much pain. The offending novice was so shocked and panic-stricken that she was on the verge of fainting. Mary reassured her that she was still very much alive and sent the novice inside to be revived with a glass of wine!

With the Sisters of Charity in Harold's Cross, service of the poor soon became a priority. A large parlour in the convent was allocated for evening lessons for the many young factory girls who had little in the way of education. Mary remarked: 'It is sweet music to my heart, to listen to these poor girls being taught to know and love God.'

The sisters also visited the sick poor daily in the impoverished dwellings in Francis Street. When the new infant school was opened, Mary experienced great joy in hearing the lessons chanted by the children in their classrooms.

Another cause of joy for Mary was watching the setting sun from her bedroom window. This sight so lifted her spirit that she would often exclaim: 'What must be the glory of Heaven?'

On one occasion Mary saw from her window a poor man being turned away. She was very distressed and asked the workman who had sent the man away to call him back and send him to the convent door, and said: 'That poor man may yet open Heaven for me.' In her teachings Mary stressed the importance of respect for the poor and she always instructed her sisters never to leave a poor person waiting in the hall nor to send an answer through a third person. She would often say that 'in them we serve Christ, as they bear the image of God'.

Mary was to spend thirteen years in Harold's Cross and all this time, despite increasing pain and disability, she was involved, as far as possible, in the life and work of the congregation. Towards the beginning of 1858 Mary became seriously ill and was barely able to hold the 'poor lame pen'. When people sympathised with her in her constant pain, Mary would reply: 'God's will. Amen.'

On the eve of her death, the sisters in Donnybrook sent a messenger to enquire after her health. Mary's thoughts were only for the poor lady who had walked all the way and she asked that a new pair of boots be given to her. Then, remembering that the next day was the feast of St Mary Magdalene, when the ladies in Donnybrook would be celebrating their feast day, Mary told the sisters: 'If I die tomorrow, do not tell the poor penitents until the day after, as it would spoil their pleasure.' These are Mary's last recorded words.

The following day, 22 July 1858, Mary died at 3 p.m., having received holy communion a few hours earlier.

Mary's funeral Mass was celebrated in Donnybrook chapel and attended by a large number of Church dignitaries, lay people and the sisters. A group of men representing Dublin workmen asked if they could have the honour of carrying Mary's coffin to her grave. This request was granted as Mary had ever been the advocate and benefactress of the working class.

On a Celtic cross over Mary's tomb the beautiful and very apt words are inscribed: 'I comforted the heart of the widow. I was an eye to the blind and a foot to the lame. To the poor I was a mother' (Jb 29:13–16).

In the chapel in Harold's Cross a beautiful marble statue depicting Jesus washing Peter's feet stands as a testimony to the vision and charism of Mary Aikenhead. She herself, though never to see the statue, ordered its erection to remind her sisters and followers of the

✳✳✳✳✳✳✳✳✳✳✳✳✳✳✳✳✳✳✳✳✳✳✳✳✳✳✳✳✳✳✳✳

privileged work they were called to in the 'exalted dignity' of service to the poor.

No vocation can be a more exact imitation of the Incarnate Word whilst on earth.

God was at the centre of Mary's life and her intense love of God poured itself out in her total dedication and love for the poor. This love of God, along with her ability to influence others to engage equally wholeheartedly in seeking out and helping the poverty-stricken people of her time, continues to inspire others today.

In recognition of the heroic virtues of this extraordinary and holy woman, Pope Francis issued a papal decree on 18 March 2015 declaring Mary Aikenhead 'Venerable'. This great honour conferred on Mary places her one step upwards on the path towards sainthood. That young girl of fifteen who, inspired by the plight of the poor man in the gospel story, decided to turn her back on privilege and serve the poor, has changed the world for the better – forever.

PART II

✳✳✳✳✳✳✳✳✳✳✳✳✳✳✳✳✳✳✳✳

Mary Aikenhead
The Woman

The story of Mary Aikenhead chronicles how one young woman, fired by a determination to better the lives of the poor in her day, relentlessly pursued her dream. The fire that burned in her heart, and the courage, determination and energy that drove her spirit helped her achieve what many would have considered impossible.

Mary was a holy and extraordinary woman and a closer look into the prism of her character, through which God's many-faceted light sparkled brightly, will reveal what a remarkable person she truly was.

A Great-Hearted Mother

That Mary Aikenhead was a woman of heart is beyond dispute. Mary was fortunate to have been nourished by love from her earliest years. Having to foster out their first-born must have been heart-wrenching for Mary's parents. Her father would undoubtedly have visited her frequently at the Rorkes' while doing his rounds of his patients. We can well imagine the outpouring of love Dr Aikenhead would have lavished on his little daughter, whom he must have missed so much. Mary and John Rorke similarly doted on their little charge and treated her as one of their own. Mary retained a deep and tender love for her old nurse and 'Daddy John', whom she remembered all of her life. It is notable that when writing to her friend Mother Mary de Chantal in Cork, Mary frequently asked after them and gave instructions that the sisters were to see that Mary Rorke received visits and attention in her old age.

This early experience of receiving the love of two sets of parents established Mary's character in security and love. Small wonder that she ably assumed a parental role over her three siblings when her parents died young.

It was Mary's compassionate heart which drove her to look out for the suffering poor while still a teenager, and that same heart which impelled her to accept the awesome role leading a new congregation that would specifically look after the poor.

In the early years of the congregation Mary suffered heavy losses among her young members due to the awful disease consumption. One of these first sufferers was Sr Mary Teresa Lynch. Mary took upon herself the care of this young sister and sat up with her every night for an entire month until she died. Only years later did Mary reveal to a close friend that this loss almost broke her heart.

Anecdotes from her many novices tell of Mary's motherly heart. On one occasion, a novice was given the task of carrying a leg of mutton and turnips on a large dish to the dining room. In the presence of all the sisters at the table, the novice let the dish fall and crash on the floor, and in panic fled the scene believing herself guilty of the greatest crime. Mary afterwards sent for the crying novice to come to her room where she received her with open arms and roguishly said: 'If the mutton wouldn't go to them, they could go to the mutton.' She then invited the novice to sit down, take a glass of wine and forget all about it!

Another young sister, who had severe inflammation of the eyes, was admitted to St Vincent's Hospital and had to remain in total darkness for a period of time. As she began to recover, Mary, discovering that the young lady was musical, procured a guitar for her to lessen the boredom of her long convalescence. The thoughtfulness and caring of this kind act reveals much about Mary's heart.

The heart of Mary Aikenhead encompassed everyone. We are told that if she sent a messenger to another convent, she would write instructions to the sister receiving the message not to allow the messenger to return without having had dinner. Similarly, if a messenger arrived for herself on a note of business, she would have him brought to the fire with something to eat while she prepared an answer.

Mary formed very deep friendships both inside and outside her convents. Mrs Anna Maria O'Brien, a friend from Mary's youth, was a constant caller and proved a treasure to Mary in countless ways – bringing Mary to the O'Briens' country home when she was sick, as well as travelling with the three sisters to Paris for their nursing training. The friendship between the two women endured throughout their lives, and when Mary was confined to her room for the latter years of her life, Anna Maria visited her faithfully twice a week.

Similarly, Mary formed a deep, heartfelt friendship with Dr Murray. She consulted him often about the many weighty issues concerning, among other things, new foundations. When she received notice about Dr Murray's unexpected death, she was stricken to the core.

Unable to attend his funeral, she prayed and waited with head bent alone in her room, as she had sent all the sisters but one to the funeral. This sister, on visiting her, mentioned one of the qualities of the Archbishop, and Mary suddenly burst into tears, excusing herself by saying: 'Poor nature must have its way.' No wonder that she once asked a friend: 'Did you think that I left my heart behind me when I put on the habit?'

Like Jesus in the gospel, Mary had some very special friends among her band of followers; sisters she trusted and confided in. Her love and friendship shine out in her many letters written to these great friends who were leading communities outside of Dublin. These friends she cherished till the end of her life.

Not without reason was Mary called 'the great-hearted mother' by her sisters and by those who knew her. All who visited her got a hearty welcome and a céad míle fáilte. Mary's warm-hearted personality was but the overflow of her deep and faithful love for the God to whom she pledged her life.

✳✳✳✳✳✳✳✳✳✳✳✳✳✳✳✳✳✳✳✳✳✳✳✳✳✳✳✳✳✳✳

When we know God as much as can be in this life, we should love Him too sincerely, too gratefully, to love anything created save in Him.

Friend of the Poor

Inscribed on Mary Aikenhead's tombstone are the words: 'To the poor I was a mother' (Jb 29:16). Throughout her life, Mary's heart was with the poor. From the time she played with the poor children on Eason's Hill until the day she died, the well-being of the poor was never far from her thoughts.

For Mary, the foundation of St Vincent's Hospital was the greatest joy of her life because she knew that the sick poor would receive the care they so badly lacked at that time. In order that the nursing sisters would realise their privilege in serving the sick, she drew up a method they were to apply to the smallest actions of the day. Before going on the wards each one was to pray: 'Oh, adorable Saviour, I firmly believe that Thou residest in the persons of the poor, and that in serving them I have the happiness of serving Thee.' When admitting patients, sisters were to remember: 'I was a stranger and you took me in', and when serving meals: 'I was hungry and you gave me food' (Mt 25:35). In this way she wanted her sisters to remember that in the poor 'we serve Christ, as they bear the image of God'.

As mentioned earlier, during the Asiatic cholera outbreak in Ireland in 1832 Mary, without hesitation, nominated sisters, including novices, from Stanhope Street to take on this work for the poor in the temporary hospital in Grangegorman. Her feelings for these sufferers was such that from her convent in Sandymount she wrote instructions for the sisters on how to deal with the dying, lest they frighten them with long prayers and sermons. She emphasised that in dealing with the 'poor sufferers' the examination of their consciences was to be 'entirely avoided'. Instead, a little prayer in a 'gentle tone of voice' should be recited for the patient and the sisters were to say the prayers for the dying at home in their own chapel. In an early biography we are told that Mary would often tell the sisters to make allowances for the poor, whose hardships were so great, and to deal tenderly with their feelings and even their sins. Little wonder she makes so many references to the Good Shepherd in her letters.

In many of Mary's letters her concerns revolve around the needs of the poor. When Gardiner Street school opened it brought her immense joy to know that the convent had the means to provide breakfast for the poorer children. At other times she is saddened that not enough sisters exist in the order to look after the many poor. She confesses: 'I feel very anxious in regard of the means of keeping up the mission amongst the poor sick.' Regarding the awful conditions among the poor in Clarinbridge, Galway, in the aftermath of the Famine, she writes to the sister in charge there: 'How my heart trembles at the awful state of our poor people.'

A sad incident in the early days of the congregation reveals Mary's depth of feeling for the poor in whatever circumstance. The Governor of Kilmainham prison requested the sisters to visit two young women convicted of a murder which happened during a robbery that went wrong. The two women were to be hanged. Mary went with Mother Catherine to Kilmainham and over a series of visits befriended the young women. One had lived locally in William Street and her home had received visits from the sisters in the past. On the morning of the execution Mary and Mother Catherine stayed with the two women, praying with them and offering them what comfort they could, from nine in the morning until two in the afternoon, the hour set for the execution. This was a horrendous moment for the two convicted women and no doubt traumatic for Mary and Catherine. After the execution Mary and Catherine remained for two more hours praying in the chapel. After this the sisters continued visiting the prison on Sundays, so much did Mary feel for the sufferings of the poor prisoners.

Much as Mary loved 'Our Lord's Dear Poor' in Ireland, she showed a rare generosity, as mentioned earlier, in agreeing to allow five of her sisters to set sail for Australia in 1838 to set up a foundation there which would minister to the female convicts at Parramatta prison, New South Wales. It is truly amazing that Mary made this heroic gesture, since only several months earlier she had suffered a huge loss to the congregation following the exodus of thirteen novices and three young professed sisters during a period of internal troubles. Only a deep-seated love and concern for these poor women convicts could have enabled Mary to make such a decision to send sisters on this distant and challenging new mission. Mary herself, though barely able to move due to arthritis, prepared the necessities the sisters would require to set up a new convent, including many requisites for a school which she dearly hoped would benefit the children.

In her later years Mary's prolonged illness and disablement prevented her from directly serving the poor, but confinement did not mean she abandoned them. Every spare moment was spent addressing letters, folding papers or making little fancy boxes as prizes for the poor. She personally wrote thousands of begging letters to businesses and well-off people appealing for funds to maintain the various services for the poor. Not without reason did she state: 'We have undertaken to be real beggars for the sake of His own poor.' Her interest in giving employment to as many poor people as she could afford was well known and it is documented that she always enquired into their family circumstances to ascertain whether there were children who needed schooling or other means of support. On one occasion a sister broke the sad news to her of a mistake in the erection of part of a particular building which would entail pulling down a wall and rebuilding it. Mary was delighted, saying it would enable her to give more work to the poor men and God would surely supply the means of paying them!

To the poor, Mary was indeed a mother and a true friend, and she never tired of reminding her sisters that the angels might well envy their high privilege in being 'the vowed servants of the poor'.

> *It is God's own work;*
> *God can do it, and He will do it.*

Centred on God

Do all in your power to live in the actual
presence of God.

Almost every letter written by Mary over the last decades of her life – and there are almost one thousand still in existence – is laced with constant references to God. These letters reveal a woman who had both an absolute trust in God and a desire only to 'promote His Divine Honour and Glory'. It is clear from her writings that she lived and breathed conscious of God's presence.

'Perfect conformity with His Holy Will' was like a mantra that Mary believed should be in the heart of every Sister of Charity. She viewed every difficulty and challenge to be 'the Holy appointments of Our Heavenly Father ... who knows what is best for our real good', and she constantly encouraged the sisters to view every happening in this light. Mary was never known to complain or murmur when faced with trying difficulties. On one occasion, writing to a sister, she mentioned a very severe difficulty she faced regarding St Vincent's Hospital, saying: 'When I open to you the state of difficulties, it is only to your own self, and it is on the understanding of not (even for one second of time) allowing anything like complaint to pass through my mind.' As usual, she referred all to the 'all wise Father' who knows what is best for his 'poor blind children'. Accepting God's will was central to Mary's spirituality and she repeatedly urged her sisters to accept cheerfully whatever God laid out for them. A constant prayer on her lips was: 'God's will. Amen.'

Mary was a woman of prayer. She strongly believed in the power of prayer. In one letter she wrote that 'we must pray, pray and faint not' when a situation is causing anxiety. Some of her letters contain spontaneous prayers as she poured out her heart to God to bless and protect all she has undertaken on behalf of the poor.

In her letters to community leaders she frequently asked the sisters for prayers for the poor. These would include prayers for the children preparing for first communion and confirmation in the schools, for good attendance at the evening and Sunday schools for the factory girls, for the support of 'our dear holy missions', for a young eighteen-year-old soldier facing execution for a rash action ending in murder, for the poor people in the country suffering want during the Famine.

For the young sisters in the noviciate, Mary was ever-begging in prayers that they would become steady and good religious, fit to minister to the poor. When a sister was dying, Mary would be sure to send letters to all the communities asking for prayers for their final journey. Following their death, she would again send out the mortuary card seeking prayers for the deceased. Once she got much annoyed with a community leader who had failed to alert her when a sister was seriously ill, thus depriving the sister of the aid of prayers in her final illness. Mary also insisted that the deceased sisters be remembered annually in prayer on their anniversaries.

The benefactors of the congregation were held in special regard by Mary and she stressed it was the duty of every sister always to pray for their benefactors. She established that Mass would be offered annually for the departed founders and benefactors of St Vincent's Hospital. To the present day, Mary's injunction that prayers be said for benefactors of the congregation, living and dead, is still continued in the evening prayer in each community of the Religious Sisters of Charity.

The road of life seldom runs smoothly, and difficulties occurred from time to time when people did not appreciate what the sisters were doing for the poor. Mary is most discreet in her letters not to mention the offenders; instead, she asks for prayers for them 'to avert the Divine Judgements even from the guilty – for all are the children of our Father and each soul was purchased by the Sacred blood of Jesus Christ'. On another occasion she writes: 'We ought to pray for those who exercise us. Amen.'

Mary had a deep devotion to prayer before the Blessed Sacrament. She was never so happy as when she learned that the Blessed Sacrament was 'enthroned' in each new convent. Mary prayed whenever she could before the Blessed Sacrament, even when it meant dragging her painful limbs up and down the many stairs in St Vincent's to reach the chapel. She wrote with great delight to her friend in Cork to say that in St Vincent's Hospital chapel, three hours of adoration of the Blessed Sacrament took place for the sole purpose of obtaining graces for all employed or to be employed in the hospital. Benediction of the Blessed Sacrament was a devotion dearly cherished by Mary and having it every evening in the convent chapel gave her great joy. She once wrote that not having 'the usual Benediction in the evenings is a great loss to me'. We remember that it was in her late childhood that the experience of Benediction reignited Mary's interest in the Catholic faith.

Mary believed that 'prayer works miracles'. Her advice to a sister who was undergoing a most complex situation in her ministry was to 'go to Him in the poor little Throne of His love' and talk to him freely seeking his advice, while reminding her: 'We walk in the Divine Presence.' She often reminded the sisters that the eternal one is 'Our Father and Dear Spouse' so how could he not listen and respond. Here we get an insight into Mary's own familiar and intimate relationship with God, whom she again and again refers to as 'Our Heavenly Father' and in whose presence she no doubt walked herself.

Scriptural images abound in her letters, which is evidence that she loved the word of God and pondered it often. One of her favourite sayings from scripture which she used again and again and which she offered as advice to sisters in trying circumstances was: 'Oh Lord, increase my Faith' (Lk 17:5). She constantly prayed that prayer and begged sisters to pray it for herself. She often reminded the sisters to be like the five wise virgins having their lamps trimmed with the oil of love in readiness for the call of the Lord (Mt 25:1–13). She frequently advised them to live by the maxim: 'Learn of me to be meek and humble of heart' (Mt 11:29) and to be loving towards each other in community, because Christ promised 'the cup of cold water' would not lose its reward (Mt 10:42). Her confidence in God's love is evident in her comment that like the 'poor little chicken' we should come humbly to Christ and 'be certain of loving shelter' (Lk 13:34).

Mary's heart was full of gratitude to God at all times regardless of the situation. Many of her letters expressed words of thanks for favours received, and more often for crosses which came her way. She thanked 'the Divine Goodness for many mercies'. She felt grateful to the Heavenly Father for charity given to the poor, for an increase in novices, for a dying sister who is well prepared for her final journey. Her short prayer, 'Amen', was forever on her lips and it signified her total acquiescence to whatever God sent her, good or bad.

From her letters we can infer that Mary lived in an atmosphere of prayer. This is borne out by her writing to her friend in Cork saying that 'the state of affairs in Cork' was so much on her mind that she added an 'Amen' every quarter of an hour to her prayers for the situation. Mary, however, was not above censuring a sister who undertook a 'long exercise of vocal prayer' to Our Lady in spite of holding an onerous position of activity in the community. She stoutly stated that one Hail Mary said with devotion would be 'just as pleasing to our ever Blessed Mother'.

Our Lady held a special place in Mary's heart. The rosary was her favourite devotion and this surely stemmed from her early days praying the rosary with her foster parents. Mary loved the Magnificat and always prayed it in thanksgiving after confession. The Salve Regina was prayed for obtaining favours from God and the Memorare when times were tough. Mary was one of the first to introduce into Ireland the devotions for the month of May in honour of Our Lady. She chose the prayers for the devotions and introduced the practice of schoolchildren processing around the grounds of the convent during May singing hymns in honour of Mary, a practice which still exists in the primary schools of the Religious Sisters of Charity.

Mary selected the Feast of the Assumption as the patronal feast of the congregation and it is clear in her letters that she dearly loved this feast. Each new convent was given a title of Our Lady and the feast day of each was to be celebrated in the community. Mary's childlike love for Our Lady is aptly summed up in her own words in a letter to Mother Mary Lucy on the eve of the Assumption in 1836: 'You will not fail to obtain most precious graces for yourself and others, if you have recourse to our ever blessed Queen and dear mother, with the love and confidence of an affectionate and devoted child.'

Bank of Divine Providence

God will settle everything; the work is His;
He will bring all things right in the end.

Confidence in God and courage to dare the impossible were but two branches emanating from Mary's deep-rooted trust in the bank of Divine Providence. Her trust in God's Providence was severely tested when she faced almost insurmountable odds in founding a hospital for the sick poor. Obstacles abounded as people she had hoped to depend on poured scorn on her lack of prudence, as they saw it, in starting such a large venture without the necessary funds. Adding to this, complaints were made that already too many calls were being made on the public for charity. These difficulties only served to deepen Mary's trust and conviction that all was 'God's own work' and she continued bravely onwards, trusting in what she said was her only resource, the bank of Divine Providence. Her trust was rewarded, for as workmen got busy with transforming the building into a hospital, benefactors began to support the project. Ever after, Mary always alluded to St Vincent's Hospital as a continual 'miracle of Divine Providence'.

Following a fire at the hospital ten years later, Mary wrote to her friend in Cork telling of her relief that none of the sisters or the 'poor patients' suffered any ill effects, all of which she attributed to the protection of 'our Merciful Almighty Father'. She asked for prayers of thanksgiving 'for all the wonderful protection of Almighty Providence over our dear congregation wherever it exists'.

On several occasions Mary referred to the bounty of Divine Providence when money appeared unexpectedly in support of the poor. She thanked 'our Heavenly Father' for twenty-seven pounds received and stated that 'it matters little by what means we and those around us are supported, all comes from His Almighty Providence'.

She advised against 'fretful anxiety' over lack of funds, as this would make sisters unfit to 'promote the interests of the poor'.

Mary counselled against anxiety on another occasion when funds, which were promised for the establishment of the convent in Lady Lane, Waterford, appeared to be in jeopardy. She told the sister in charge of the convent: 'do not fear, all will go well' provided she practise 'entire dependence on His sweet Providence'.

Business matters were also placed under the care of Divine Providence and Mary, much relieved that a matter of public concern in Cork was satisfactorily concluded, saw this as 'the truly miraculous interference of His holy Providence'. The turn of events in this situation, after much prayer, concluded in favour of the poor and appeared to Mary as nothing short of a miracle.

During the terrible hardships of the Famine years, Mary asked all the sisters to unite in praying for 'our daily bread'. She lamented the trying times all were experiencing throughout the country, and this amidst talk of worse to come. She, however, believed that God was over all and already sustained 'our Charitable Institutions' which was 'evidently a miracle of His adorable Providence'. Mary viewed all the charitable donations which sustained the works for the poor as the generous bounty of a 'truly miraculous Friend Almighty Providence'.

Mary taught the sisters to do their 'little best' to support the poor and then leave the rest to God, depending on his 'sweet Providence'. Even during the most worrying times, when funds were low, she kept trusting in her 'imperishable bank' and was seldom disappointed. She couldn't bear to see sisters anxious or fretting over money matters and she would state: 'Why distrust the sweet Providence of God by wanting to have more than we actually require for present use?' Neither did she want her sisters to sit back and do nothing; they were to provide the five loaves and two fishes and allow the Lord to multiply their efforts. She taught them to say with confidence: 'I can do all things in Him who strengthens me.' This was the motto by which she herself lived and which always motivated her in risking undertakings she thought would give glory to God. This daring conviction in pushing out boundaries for the sake of the poor was not without cost, and Mary alluded to this in a letter when she disclosed that she has had her share of 'the oppositions of the world and of the old enemy'. But, like St Paul, she knows who it is that she has put her trust in (2 Tm 1:12), and can confidently claim: 'Our work would be overpowering were we to view all in any other light than as God's own work, and entirely depending on the Miraculous aid of His Almighty Providence.'

It is clear that Mary had an intimate, trusting relationship with her Heavenly Father, as she liked to call him, and this trust enabled her to labour as if everything depended on her, while at the same time trusting that all depended on God.

> *Exercise unlimited confidence in Him,*
> *who will never allow you to be*
> *tried above your strength.*

She Touched the Sky yet Trod the Earth

Although Mary's letters reveal a woman steeped in an awareness of God's pervading presence, she had her feet firmly planted on the ground of human experience.

Mary's early years at home as manager of her own household meant she was trained well in domestic matters, and she also possessed a natural gift for business acumen. We see these qualities emerge in her letters when she wrote to Sr Francis Magdalen who was in charge of the establishment of the new convent at Preston, England. She requested in writing 'some little sketch of each floor and dimensions of each room, where windows are, or at least how many'. Mary planned every detail from her wheelchair and had a clear picture of the interior of each new convent, building or schoolroom. She was always particular about fresh air being available to the sisters, so windows and their location were of utmost importance so as to get as much ventilation as possible. She advised that each convent should have a 'little garden or place to retire to for air and exercise'. Mary lived at a time when tuberculosis was rampant and had caused severe losses among the young sisters in the early days of the congregation; hence her anxiety for space and fresh air. Other household needs in a new house were also of concern. She sent to Clonmel 'linen to bleach' and 'sixteen pairs of sheets with pillow covers'. She also sent a roll of check to make bed covers: 'It is excellent, 6 1/2d the yard.' Mary was certainly grounded in matters of day-to-day living; be it the technicalities of architecture or the cost of cotton, nothing was beyond her interest.

Practicalities about the running of a house were not above mentioning in her letters. In an age when health and safety issues were not enshrined in law, she was quick to offer instructions regarding precautions to be observed where fire was concerned. Advice was to be obtained from wise and experienced persons regarding fire safety – and only then was the building to be placed under the protection of St Joseph! Mary advised the insuring of convents and 'establishments connected with them'. She stated: 'St Joseph is truly an efficient "Insurance Officer", but we are also bound to observe human means when such are afforded to us.' She even instructed the sisters to be 'in bed on time' and to take 'care about gas and other lights and fire'. However, Mary, ever practical, was not rigid around rules and regulations. Writing to the sister in charge in Preston, she stipulated certain modes of action, but then remembered circumstances there may be different from those in Dublin, and so she wisely advised flexibility, saying: 'Remember that in Rome it is better to act as folk do in Rome.' Wise government, not whim or personal inclination, was to prevail when engaging in 'functions in favour of the poor' in whatever place the sisters were in ministry.

Mary was a shrewd observer of human nature and was adept at analysing the workings of the mind. She was full of common sense and practical wisdom. She instructed the novices on visiting the poor to walk through the streets in silence, but not to be so lost in God as not to see where they were going! She wanted them to use their common sense at all times. And, while she wanted them to try to live always in the presence of God, she abhorred false piety. Her humour is evident in her statement: 'I don't want my nuns holy pokers!' She was also heard to say: 'We don't want children here, we want women who have sense and know how to use it.'

In dealing with the sisters, Mary was not so naive as to expect perfection from each one. She understood the weaknesses of human nature. She once counselled a community leader to be more tolerant of imperfections in her sisters, reminding her that God demands only 'our reasonable service'. Mary believed that in spite of imperfections each sister is 'most dear to the Sacred Heart' who, while on earth, supported the weak ones and loved them. Another time, she advised, 'Find fault and leave it there', because to go back over past mistakes or to show anger would sour human relationships. It was widely known that Mary herself, although firm and outspoken when necessary, after a reprimand very wisely went on to other more pleasant issues in a gentle tone and never in the future referred to the topic again. She understood the workings of human nature and, like St Francis de Sales, was aware that a spoon of honey captivates more hearts than a glass of vinegar.

Mary often advised her sisters to be wise and discreet. Where differences of opinion arose, she advised they were not to 'get into altercations with people', as this merely served to exacerbate the situation. She believed a 'well-timed silence' paves the way for a later 'well-timed word of explanation'. She counselled 'be mild', as this will disarm the troublemaker.

Mary's sensitivity of soul shone through, especially in trying times, such as when untrue rumours were circulating about the congregation. She believed every effort to contradict the untruths would only make matters worse: 'We cannot assert truth without proving others to have

✳✳✳✳✳✳✳✳✳✳✳✳✳✳✳✳✳✳✳✳✳✳✳✳✳✳✳✳✳✳✳✳

uttered the contrary.' Here we see both her wisdom and her consideration towards those in the wrong.

To those inclined to depression, Mary's advice was: be cheerful. She knew well how despondent her friend in Cork could become when troubles abound, and advised her to raise her mind above dwelling on the problems either 'public or domestic', as this was the very point 'where the enemy loves to fish'. Making acts of faith and confidence in God would dispel the 'illusions'. She warned: 'Low spirits and dread of evil to ourselves or congregation, or even to the Church, are actually the beginning of despair.' When training the novices Mary would teach them always to remain cheerful and joyful and to serve God and others with a cheerful heart. She would often say: 'We ought not let sadness or anxiety banish joy from our lives.'

From the letters of Mary Aikenhead and from the writings of the sisters who knew her well, we see a woman possessed of spiritual depth, practical wisdom, humanity and sound common sense. She is never at a loss to make

****

suggestions about the practical running of a house; she gives sound advice on dealing with the vagaries of human nature; she offers encouragement and support when necessary, and indeed a reprimand when it is called for. Her life was a busy round of prayer, letter writing and meetings with a variety of visitors: from prelates to businessmen to sisters and to the poor. But Mary managed to balance all, since, like St Ignatius, she aimed to see God in all things, and her heart knew no separation between God and the things of God.

Our work would be overpowering
were we to view all in any other light
than in God's own work.

Patient Sufferer

*I must be willing to suffer, whilst Our Lord
is pleased to leave me in this life.*

Mary Aikenhead's life's work – her involvement with the poor, her training of novices, her establishment of new foundations and her astounding and prolific letter writing – might well mask the reality of a life spent in almost unremitting physical suffering. A detailed reading of her letters and early biographies reveals the extent of such suffering.

In the early 1830s, Mary's health, which had been failing for some time, broke down and necessitated complete rest and fresh air. She moved to Sandymount convent and there she underwent a series of drastic remedies prescribed by a physician who mistakenly diagnosed her with 'internal cancer'. This physician prescribed large doses of dangerous drugs which caused Mary intense suffering, and resulted in damaging her health in a way that would leave her quite an invalid for the last twenty-seven years of her life. Thanks to the pharmacist who, recognising the severity of the drugs, refused to dispense them, telling the sisters 'Rev. Mother is being poisoned', Mary was transferred to the care of Dr O'Ferrall who diagnosed the real cause of Mary's problem – severe inflammation of the spine. In today's parlance, Mary was suffering from acute, inflamed arthritis.

Mary was only forty-four and for the next few years she was confined to her room, a helpless and suffering invalid. She was required to lie in the same position for a long period of time, and when she did sit up her head had to be supported with a cushion. She confided: 'I cannot stand without intense pain nor move without suffering more than anyone could know, all this from the back, and when fatigued the head becomes badly affected.'

✳✳✳✳✳✳✳✳✳✳✳✳✳✳✳✳✳✳✳✳✳✳✳✳✳✳✳✳✳✳✳✳

Under the able care of Dr O'Ferrall, Mary made progress and was able to get out on occasions to visit or do business at one of her convents.

It is interesting to note that during this time of pain and inaction, Mary, in the midst of many other pressing concerns, had been putting into place plans for the setting up of St Vincent's Hospital, as well as providentially procuring the loyal services of Dr O'Ferrall for this new venture.

When St Vincent's opened, Mary moved there from Sandymount and had her bedroom-cum-office at the top of the building. Here, in spite of being so often indisposed, she patiently received the many visitors calling on her for advice or on business matters. At this time Mary suffered much from her spine and she wrote to her close friend, Mother Mary de Chantal: 'May you not have to suffer as much bodily trial as it pleased our all wise and ever merciful Father to appoint for me.' She went on to say that not for one moment would she wish otherwise for herself than according to 'His Most Holy Will'.

That Mary suffered almost permanently from pain and headaches is evidenced in her letters where she responds to enquiries about her health. In one letter she admitted to interrupting her writing as she had received a painful remedy from a doctor who gave her 'copious application of his cupping glass' which caused pain and blisters. The result was excessive pain to her back and head, so much so that writing, for Mary, was easier 'than of speaking to dictate'.

Another development in Mary's health meant that not alone was her spine affected, but her right arm was painfully swollen with 'redness of the fingers, hand and arm'. Even her leg became swollen, so that she had to avail of a wheelchair. Given her alarming deterioration in health, Mary moved in 1845 to Harold's Cross where she could avail of the benefits of the fresh country air.

In Harold's Cross Mary enjoyed a short respite in suffering due to her occasional outdoor expeditions in her wheelchair – and also perhaps due to extra rest, as she had a little more freedom from the constant visitors who had called on her in St Vincent's. Nevertheless, she continued to suffer greatly. We get a glimpse into the drastic remedies used in those days when she told Mother Mary Ignatius in a letter in 1849 that she had been very poorly, but 'the leeches and blister of last evening have greatly relieved the pain of the ear'.

Although Mary continued to write many letters, it often caused her intense pain to take up her 'poor lame pen'. In 1853, when she was sixty-six years old, she wrote to her close friend excusing her terrible scribble arising from her hand and arm, which she said are in such a state of pain that she was 'unable to use the pen for some days'. From about this time onwards until her death in 1858, Mary continued to suffer patiently. We are told that in her final months her spinal muscles were so weak they could not support her head so that it sank forward on her chest. During mealtimes a sister had to hold Mary's head back so she could take the food. Through it all Mary's prayer was: 'God's will, Amen.'

Mary believed, as taught by St Ignatius, founder of the

Jesuits, that 'sickness is no less the gift of God than health' and this determined her approach to her sufferings.

In a letter to one of her sisters she stated: 'We must ... receive the visitation of bodily infirmity as a precious mark of the Divine favour.' She could say regarding her suffering: 'I do not wish to be otherwise than I am' except in regard of 'spiritual improvement'. She never prayed for an end to her suffering as she believed that God had ordained everything. Neither was she ever heard to complain about her sufferings, as she always wanted what God wanted. One of the sisters who knew Mary heard her say often that great good could be done for the good of others and for God's glory by those who are themselves sufferers.

It is quite extraordinary that in spite of chronic ill-health and suffering, Mary was able to achieve so much for the glory of God with all the complexities and challenges entailed in setting up and governing a new congregation; it is equally extraordinary how patiently and lovingly she endured her suffering. God's glory and

✳✳✳✳✳✳✳✳✳✳✳✳✳✳✳✳✳✳✳✳✳✳✳✳✳✳✳✳✳✳✳

God's will were paramount for Mary, and her love and fidelity with regard to both, through all her sufferings and endeavours on behalf of the suffering poor, will surely forever inspire her many faithful followers.

Opposition from Within

It would be rare to find a founder or foundress for whom great enterprises were accomplished without having to undergo many obstacles designed to undermine their efforts. When a great work is undertaken for God, usually there is opposition between the light and the darkness.

Fr St Leger, a Jesuit friend and long-standing advisor of Mary, once wrote to her saying: 'May you never know by experience the curse of religious persons differing in their opinion from their Constitutions.' Unfortunately, Mary was to suffer severe trials in the early years of the congregation through precisely such persons.

Her first trouble began in 1824. Mary had gone from Stanhope Street to Porterstown to help look after two young sisters suffering from tuberculosis. During her absence, one of the community in Stanhope Street, Sr Mary Peter, began to make her authority felt and tried to instil in the hearts of the community disapproval of the constitutions which she considered too strict and not suitable for sisters engaged in active work with the poor. Since the constitutions had not yet been confirmed by Rome, she had hoped to have aspects changed before the final approval. On Mary's return, she discovered the turmoil created by Sr Mary Peter, who was not willing to change her views. She continued to try to sow seeds of discontent in the community, so that Mary had no option but to call in Archbishop Murray for dialogue with the disgruntled sister. Even this intervention had not the required effect, and eventually, after causing further disturbance in the community, Sr Mary Peter decided to leave the congregation and join another community.

This period of suffering was so weighty for Mary that she later confided in a letter to a friend that only prayer before the Blessed Sacrament carried her through this painful episode.

About ten years later, Mary was to undergo a further trial which almost shook the very foundations of the congregation. This trouble came in the form of a Miss Elizabeth Bodenham, a member of an aristocratic English family, who asked for admission to the Sisters of Charity. She was forty years old when she joined the congregation, a highly intellectual and literary person who had studied the Bible and Church history as well as authoring some religious books.

Throughout Mary's letters we read on several occasions her thoughts on the personality and character traits of the young women who were applying for admission, with a view to their suitability. Her letters invariably reveal in her assessments of these novices a keen sense of human nature and a sharp, sound judgement. Unfortunately, on this occasion, Mary appears to have made a huge error of judgement in admitting Elizabeth Bodenham. Mary may have been influenced by the applicant's background in religious knowledge, as well as by the insistence with which she alleged to have no other interest but in serving the poor.

Following her profession of vows three years later, Sr

Mary Ignatius, as she was now known, was given the task of catechetical instruction to the novices, presumably because of her scriptural knowledge. Mary was no longer able to perform this task as her health had begun to deteriorate. Sr Ignatius proved to be an efficient and able instructor and was well liked by the novices.

Three years later, due to Mary's heavy involvement with the setting up of St Vincent's Hospital, she was no longer able to find the time to train the novices. She appointed Sr Mary Ignatius as Novice Mistress, feeling that she would be the most suitable person for the job, having had so much dealings with the novices through her teaching; Sr Ignatius was also appointed leader in the community.

Over a six-month period, while Mary was living in St Vincent's Hospital, Sr Mary Ignatius caused enormous damage in Stanhope Street, where she held sway over the minds and hearts of the novices and community sisters. She began to undermine Mary's authority. She referred to her setting up of the hospital as 'a little pious hallucination of Rev. Mother's' and tried to convince the sisters that nursing was beneath cultured and educated women. Preparing for a clothing ceremony of three novices, she planned a luxurious ceremony not in keeping with Mary's custom. Mary, on hearing of the event, promptly cancelled it and also discovered that the allegiance of the novices was to Sr Ignatius, who had up till now unsettled their minds with novel ideas. She made them believe that Mary was not the right leader and that they should press for an election of a new superior general to update the congregation in modern ways. Added to this, and unknown to Mary, she had made arrangements to open a foundation in Hastings, England, where she would bring the brightest of the novices to open a school for well-to-do young ladies. Mary believed firmly in the cultivation of the intellect – but never at the expense of service to the poor. Sisters of Charity were vowed to serve the poor. Mary immediately cancelled all the plans for this venture and removed Sr Ignatius from the noviceship. Unfortunately, the damage had already been done.

Thirteen novices and two young professed sisters left the congregation, one of whom was Margaret Aylward, the future foundress of the Holy Faith Sisters.

Sr Mary Ignatius was sent to the Sandymount convent, but here also she continued her intrigue, making false imputations about Mary and unsettling another young professed sister who left the congregation. Matters had come to such a head that Mary, after consulting with her council, dismissed Sr Ignatius from the congregation.

The noviceship was now reduced to nine novices since more than half had departed due to this unhappy saga. It is a testimony to Mary's trust in Divine Providence and her unwavering devotion to the service of the poor that she never faltered in her conviction, in the face of so much trouble, that Sisters of Charity were founded solely 'to promote the divine honour and the spiritual and corporal good of our Lord's poor members'.

Writing later to her friend Sr Mary de Chantal in Cork, Mary was able to say that not for 'one second' did all that had happened cause her any degree of sadness nor ever cause her to doubt God's providential care. In her letters at this time Mary never once made any comment or suggestion of animosity towards Sr Mary Ignatius. Her greatness of soul is evident when she remarked that those 'mortifying trials' and the false reports spread about her were a good antidote against the workings of self-love and secret pride which might all too easily have taken root in her soul. Through it all, Mary remained focused on God and on the preservation of the aim of the congregation, and despite the immense suffering and pruning which occurred in the order during this trial, her trust was rewarded by seeing it flourish again.

Never allow a sentiment of resentment to enter into our hearts.

Love of Vocation

That every dear Sister shall value, as the most precious jewel, and love with all the ardour of her heart, the greatest of graces bestowed on us, 'Our Religious Vocation'.

That Mary loved with all her heart the great gift of her own vocation, and highly esteemed the vocation of every sister, shines clearly through in the many letters she wrote. Mary often reminded the novices of the great glory that was theirs in being chosen to follow Christ and to imitate him, but she also reminded them that 'the habit and veil do not make the nun'. To be a Sister of Charity was a call to the 'high station as Spouses of Jesus' and their love was to be proven by deeds. To be living in God's house and serving God's poor was for Mary a most holy privilege.

In her letters Mary was constantly encouraging the sisters to study the spirit of 'our dear and holy vocation' so as to more perfectly imitate Christ. Even if the sisters were to work miracles, she believed that without the true inner spirit of 'our holy institute' all accomplishments would be but 'hay and stubble' only fit for the fire.

Mary had a horror of half-hearted religious, and therefore she strongly asserts: 'Better that we should cease to exist than that the young members should engage without due dispositions.' On the other hand, she asked that all pray that 'not one who has received a true vocation' would ever leave the congregation.

In her later years, Mary always insisted that the novices be well trained in the obligations of the vows they were about to take. She herself led by example. We are told she loved evangelical poverty. She would wear an old patched habit and her room was plain and simple. It is reported that even when sick she did not want her diet to be different from the rest of the community; 'nothing dainty or special for me' was her constant plea.

As to the vow of chastity, Mary believed that each sister was elected 'to be His own Spouse'. We are told in an early biography that 'her own heart was on fire with love of Him' and her main object in life was to teach others to love God. She impressed on the young sisters the importance of living in an awareness of God's presence and she wanted them to have hearts 'so simple as to seek God alone'. But chastity involved more than loving only God. They were to love the poor and, above all, the 'domestics of the Faith' as she called the sisters in community. She wrote: 'Charity should first shine resplendently and from our hearts, amidst our own little Communities'; otherwise all that is done on behalf of the poor will not 'entitle us to rank as true Sisters of Charity'.

Likewise, where obedience was concerned, Mary herself was most particular about obeying the directions of her ecclesiastical superior, Dr Murray. She consulted him on weighty matters concerning the congregation, and seldom on these issues did she act outside his advice and direction. During her periods of extended illness, she interpreted her vow of obedience to include the directions of the physician and infirmarian by strictly obeying their orders to rest, despite wishing to do otherwise when pressing matters awaited her attention. She wrote often to communities reminding them of the importance of the practice of obedience, and that each sister should remember that in obeying the community leader she was obeying God. Similarly, the leaders were to remember that no matter how trying their role, they were appointed by obedience and therefore 'by God Himself'.

The fourth vow – to devote their lives to the service of the poor – was to be the defining characteristic of a Sister of Charity. It was precisely because the fourth vow would enable Mary to devote her life to the service of the poor that she agreed in the first place to undertake the challenging task of leading the congregation. Mary was so intent that the young sisters should be grounded in the spirit of the congregation that she undertook herself the training of the novices. She understood that the novices were the foundation stones of the congregation, so she wanted to instil in them a deep interior life of prayer together with heartfelt compassion for the poor. She would always ask for prayers for those in the noviceship and on one occasion wrote: 'Pray for those in the noviceship that they may deserve the glorious privilege of becoming Spouses of Christ, and true Servants of His poor members.' Following the profession of novices, she asked for prayers for 'the dear ones' – who she says, have just 'become the Spouses' of Christ – that they remain faithful and never relax in their promises.

That Mary deeply lived her own promises is evident throughout her letters in her many references to 'our most high and holy vocation' and in her remembrance each year of the anniversary of her first vows. Writing in 1842 on the twenty-seventh anniversary of her profession, she stated that 'our Holy Vows' are the most pleasing offering that can be presented to God, and she mentioned her fears that, over the years, her offering may have been less perfect than it might have been.

Mary's aim always was to imitate her 'Crucified

✹✹✹✹✹✹✹✹✹✹✹✹✹✹✹✹✹✹✹✹✹✹✹✹✹✹✹✹✹

Spouse'; small wonder that she felt imperfect. She loved her vocation and, more importantly, she loved with all her heart the 'great God' who had bestowed this 'greatest gift' on her and on the congregation.

A quotation from her last letter to her best friend six months before she died is very apt:

> *Let us love the vocation to which God has elected us; it is the most perfect imitation of the God Man on earth that is in the Church.*

✳✳✳✳✳✳✳✳✳✳✳✳✳✳✳✳✳✳✳✳

Her Spirit Lives On

Shortly before she died, Mary pronounced that after her death the congregation would flourish. She led an outwardly simple life of loving service which concealed her extraordinary vision and strength of character. Underpinned by a great trust in God and a powerful imagination, Mary was determined to spread Jesus' message of showing God's unconditional love to all. Her outreach to the poor and sick of Dublin developed into a global vision. Against all kinds of odds, her courage and determination established within the Church a mission which would become the foundation for hospitals, schools, welfare services and centres of spirituality. Today, the Religious Sisters of Charity are scattered and flourishing across the globe in America, Zambia, Nigeria, Malawi, Australia, England, Scotland and, of course, in its original nursery, Ireland. The mustard seed which Mary planted has far exceeded her wildest dreams, for not only have the Religious Sisters of Charity grown and expanded within their own congregation, but they have helped new shoots spring up through assisting in the training of new congregations, such as the Columban Sisters in Ireland, the Handmaids of the Holy Child Jesus in Nigeria, the Good Samaritan Sisters in Australia, and the Sisters of Our Lady of Nazareth in Fiji. The Spirit indeed blows where it will.

The motto Mary chose for the congregation, and which embellishes the Religious Sisters of Charity crest, is *Caritas Christi Urget Nos* – the charity of Christ urges us on. It is this love of Christ that drove Mary Aikenhead, and today it impels the sisters, and the many other people associated with the congregation, to seek out the people who are least in today's world. For in spite of massive advancements in social services, together with unprecedented growth in towns and cities across the world, there are those who are left behind and on the margins, those who are made to feel worthless and totally helpless to better their lives.

Impelled still by the love of Christ and the urgency of the gospel imperative, the members of Mary Aikenhead's congregations (the second congregation being in Australia) focus their attention on social injustices, including outreach to the victims of oppression, people smuggling and slavery, abuse of women and children, poverty and homelessness.

Mary's vision was radical and unconventional. Governments and states in her time did not provide healthcare, education or services. Poverty, illiteracy and illness were widespread. Mary's sisters, imbued with her spirit, were fearless in their ministry.

Such fearlessness continues today as her congregations tackle modern-day slavery, disasters and disease. Mary visited female prisoners condemned to death in

Kilmainham Gaol. Her sisters today reach out to prisoners and detainees in prisons across four continents.

Today's Religious Sisters of Charity are also active in helping to change unjust social structures by advocating for human rights (just as Mary did in her day, for instance writing to the State Commissioners in 1833 outlining the appalling conditions of the poor) and by mobilising people power to speak out for the voiceless, especially those who are trafficked or homeless.

Like Mary in her day, the sisters are still involved throughout the congregation in education and evangelisation. In our modern and increasingly secularised society, there is a gaping need to accompany people, especially the young, on their faith journey.

Poverty wears many faces today and exists in a variety of forms, from the material to the psychological and spiritual. The poor person still lies at our gates begging for a crumb from our tables and, perhaps more than anything, begging for the crumb of a kind word and for recognition of their human dignity. And, while it may not be possible to respond financially to all those in need in today's society, wherever they minister Religious Sisters of Charity and their colleagues still provide the caring, human presence – the face of Christ – to every individual they encounter; be it in the hospital, the hospice, the home, the school, the centre or the street. They also give them a most precious commodity: their time.

Mary's life teaches us today to have faith in God and in ourselves; to dream courageous visions; to reach outward and away from preoccupations; to have compassion for human pain and brokenness; to analyse structures which are the cause of poverty; to work with others to solve problems; and to remain resolute in the face of hardship.

Our world today still challenges and confronts us. Many struggle for equality, even for the most basic of human needs, and suffering is not far from our view if we choose to recognise it. Mary's life is a fine example of how to respond to the deepest challenges which face us, and which can even test our faith.

✳✳✳✳✳✳✳✳✳✳✳✳✳✳✳✳✳✳✳✳✳✳✳✳✳✳✳✳✳✳✳

Mary Aikenhead lived a holy life; a life given in total dedication to God and to the needs of the poor. She was a powerful influence and through her work engaged others to seek out and help the poverty-stricken and neglected people of their time. Consequently, Pope Francis, acknowledging her heroic virtues on 18 March 2015, conferred on Mary the title 'Venerable Mary Aikenhead', thus placing her on the path towards sainthood.

Yes, today, the spirit of Mary Aikenhead lives on: it lives on in every healthcare, pastoral and educational ministry associated with the sisters; it lives on in every person who loves and promotes the charism of Mary; and it lives on in every Religious Sister of Charity who has vowed her life to the service of God and to his needy members.

The gift of Mary Aikenhead to the Church and to the world is a living gift because it is the gift of the gospel: the gift of love. And it is a free gift, available to those who want to be involved with us in the great enterprise of loving as Jesus did, of loving as Mary Aikenhead did.

Bibliography

Blake, Donal S., cfc, *Mary Aikenhead (1787–1858) Servant of the Poor: Founder of the Religious Sisters of Charity* (Private Publication, 2001).

Butler, Katherine, RSC, *They Called Her Mary* (Earlsford Press, 1982).

Flanagan, Mary Padua, RSC, ed., *Letters of Mary Aikenhead* (Longmans, Green & Co., 1914).

Flanagan, Mary Padua, RSC, *The Life and Work of Mary Aikenhead* (Longmans, Green & Co., 1925).

Homily Notes of Most Rev. Diarmuid Martin, Archbishop of Dublin, *Mass to Give Thanks for the Declaration on the Heroic Virtues of the Venerable Mary Aikenhead* (Church of the Holy Family, Aughrim Street, 26 April 2015).

Padberg, John W., SJ, ed., *The Constitutions of the Society of Jesus and their Complementary Norms: A Complete English Translation of the Official Latin Texts* (Institute of Jesuit Sources, 1996).

Religious Sisters of Charity/Sisters of Charity of Australia, Brochure: *Venerable Mary Aikenhead: A Saint for Our Time* (Private Publication).

Atkinson, Sarah, *Mary Aikenhead – Her Life, her Work, and her Friends* (M. H. Gill & Son; Burns and Oates, 1882).

The Jerusalem Bible, Popular Edition (Darton, Longman and Todd, 1974).